# vision board
## CLIP ART BOOK
## FOR MEN.

300+ elements
BY KALISHIA WINSTON

 # YOUR FREE GIFTS

As a way of saying thanks for your purchase,
I want to offer you two free bonuses:

### FREE GIFT #1:

### "86 QUICK & EASY STRATEGIES FOR SAVING MONEY" EBOOK

*Discover 86 practical and easy-to-implement strategies to save money, budget wisely, and achieve your financial goals. This eBook is a valuable resource for securing your financial future.*

### FREE GIFT #2:

### "CREATING YOUR DREAM LIFE WITH YOUR OWN VISION BOARD" COURSE

*Unlock the potential within you and start manifesting your aspirations with my exclusive vision board course. Set clear intentions and turn your dreams into reality.*

## SIGN UP FOR MY EMAIL NEWSLETTER TO GET INSTANT ACCESS:
# MEN.KALISHIAWINSTON.COM

You will also get weekly tips, free book giveaways, discounts, and so much more.

All of these bonuses are completely free and come with no strings attached. You do not need to provide any personal information except for your email address.

DIGITAL DETOX

# Seek Balance

## MEDITATION

**DETERMINATION.**

**FITNESS**

# S♥ULMATE

*Weathering Storms Together*

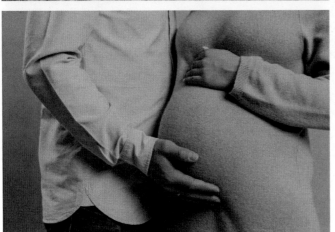

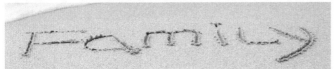

SUPER DAD

# FRIENDSHIP

# Brotherhood

WANDERLUST

TRAVEL AROUND THE WORLD

TIME MANAGEMENT

HU$TLE COMMITMENT AMBITION

PASSION Create

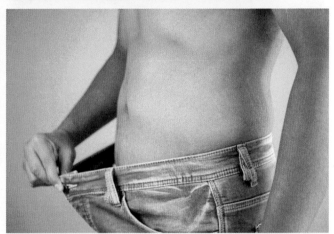

NO
STOP
SUGAR

DIET

WELLNESS

LIVE HEALTHY
LIFESTYLE

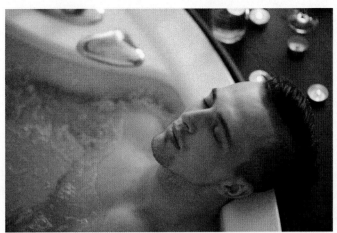

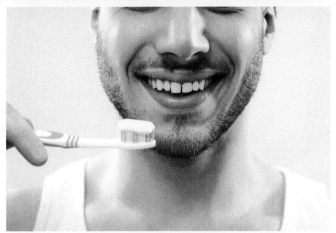

SKIN CARE

TONER

cream

Health ∿→
BEGINS
WITH
Self care

TAKE
CARE
OF
YOUR
SELF

# ECO HOUSE
## REAL ESTATE

| CAREER | BUSINESS | HOME |
|---|---|---|
| CREATIVITY | WEALTH | GOALS |
| GYM | FUN | HEALTH |
| DREAMS | FINANCE | SAVINGS |
| SPIRITUALITY | MINDSET | FAMILY |
| EDUCATION | HOBBIES | PERSONAL GROWTH |
| MANIFEST | SCHOOL | TRAVEL |
| GIVING BACK | SELF CARE | LOVE |
| PETS | MENTAL HEALTH | COMMUNITY |
| ADVENTURE | KIDS | FAITH |
| LIFESTYLE | SELF LOVE | FRIENDS |

| | | |
|---|---|---|
| things to see | focus | luxury |
| dream job | independent | progress |
| successful | my dream life | believe |
| wedding | goals to meet | take risks |
| dreamer | less screen time | study |
| boss | calm | gratitude |
| every day | precision | live simply |
| profit | things to try | love your life |
| experiences | beautiful | outdoors |
| imagine | hope | grateful |
| joy | explore | get it |

| | | |
|---|---|---|
| I EMBRACE SUCCESS | I TAKE MY GOALS SERIOUSLY | I HONOR MY NEED TO REST AND RECHARGE |
| I CHOOSE TO TAKE RESPONSIBILITY FOR MY OWN HAPPINESS | I RELEASE MY NEED TO COMPARE MYSELF TO OTHERS | I AM FREE TO CREATE MY OWN REALITY |
| I RELEASE MY ATTACHMENT TO EVERYTHING THAT NO LONGER SERVES ME | I AM CALM IN THE FACE OF CONFLICT | I AM PRODUCTIVE AND FOCUSED ON RESULTS |
| I WILL CREATE A HEALTHY LIFESTYLE FOR MYSELF | I WILL BECOME AN INSPIRING MAN | I DO MY BEST EACH AND EVERYDAY |

I AM READY TO SHOW THE WORLD WHO I AM AND WHAT I HAVE TO OFFER

DON'T WISH FOR IT, WORK FOR IT

| | | |
|---|---|---|
| SEOUL | HAWAII | THAILAND |
| ROME | ISTANBUL | FRANCE |
| VIETNAM | SWITZERLAND | BAHAMAS |
| USA | LOS ANGELES | FIJI |
| SYDNEY | NEW ZEALAND | BALI |
| JORDAN | GERMANY | SOUTH AFRICA |
| ISRAEL | TOKYO | INDIA |
| TULUM | IRAN | DENMARK |
| NEPAL | NORWAY | PORTUGAL |
| EGYPT | BANFF | SOUTH AMERICA |
| LONDON | PERU | MEXICO |

| | | |
|---|---|---|
| AFRICA | ITALY | SWEDEN |
| GREECE | CUBA | IRELAND |
| CROATIA | MOROCCO | AUSTRALIA |
| MALDIVES | SPAIN | BORA BORA |
| PARIS | BERLIN | CANADA |
| RIO DE JANEIRO | CHINA | ASIA |
| EUROPE | JAPAN | SCOTLAND |
| NEW YORK | PRAGUE | HONG KONG |
| AMSTERDAM | DUBAI | CANCUN |
| BARCELONA | LISBON | BUENOS AIRES |
| SAN FRANCISCO | DUBLIN | BANGKOK |

## ✈ BOARDING PASS

FROM:     TO:

PASSENGER NAME:     →

_____

BOARDING TIME:     DATE:

_____

SEAT:     FLIGHT:

**For manifesting purposes only. Not for use to board a flight at the airport.**

## 🏛 BANK OF THE UNIVERSE

DATE: _____

PAY TO THE
ORDER OF:

_____    $ _____

_____    DOLLARS

FOR: _____

00000000 ⊩56    00000000 296 456    **For manifesting purposes only.**

## SPECIAL TICKET
# VIP GUEST

Event:

Exclusively for:

**For the sole purpose of manifesting your desires.**

Date:

Location:

ADMIT ONE VIP GUEST    VIP PASS

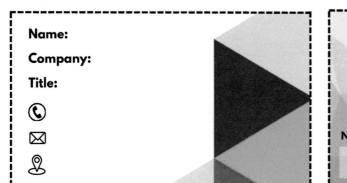

**Name:**

**Company:**

**Title:**

📞

✉

📍

# GOLD MEMBER

**VIP Club Name**

Name

**member no.**
**123-456-789**

# THANK YOU

*"Helping others is the way we help ourselves."*
*-Oprah Winfrey*

Have you ever given without expecting anything in return? If you have, you are aware of the tremendous rewards that can come from helping others. Not because it makes you a better person, but because it makes you feel good to know that you were able to improve someone else's life in some small way.

I want to give you this chance and ask you for a favor. In order for me to accomplish my mission of inspiring my readers to live their best lives, I first have to reach them. And the majority of people do evaluate a book based on its reviews. So, could you please take 3 minutes to post your honest review of this book on Amazon? With your help, this book will reach more people and assist them in achieving their goals and dreams. Just find this book on Amazon and write a few short words (or long words, I won't judge).

P.S. If you believe this book will benefit someone you know, please let them know about it too.

To your success,

Kalishia Winston

Made in the USA
Las Vegas, NV
03 January 2025

15714590R00031